THE SAN ANTONIO SPURS

Sloan MacRae

PowerKiDS
press.

New York

Published in 2010 by The Rosen Publishing Group, Inc.
29 East 21st Street, New York, NY 10010

First Edition

Editor: Amelie von Zumbusch
Book Design: Greg Tucker
Photo Researcher: Jessica Gerweck

Photo Credits: Cover (Tim Duncan) Brian Bahr/Getty Images; cover (background) by Mirac Aktepe; cover, p. 5 Chris Graythen/Getty Images; cover, p. 13 Jerry Wachter/Sports Imagery/Getty Images; cover, p. 17 Garrett W. Ellwood/Getty Images; p. 7 Nathaniel S. Butler/NBAE/Getty Images; pp. 9, 22 (top) NBA Photo Library/NBAE/Getty Images; p. 11 Dick Raphael/NBAE/Getty Images; pp. 15, 22 (middle) D. Clarke Evans/NBAE/Getty Images; p. 19 Layne Murdoch/NBAE/Getty Images; pp. 21, 22 (bottom) Liam Kyle/NBAE/Getty Images.

Library of Congress Cataloging-in-Publication Data

MacRae, Sloan.
  The San Antonio Spurs / Sloan MacRae. — 1st ed.
      p. cm. — (America's greatest teams)
  Includes index.
  ISBN 978-1-4042-8133-2 (library binding) — ISBN 978-1-4358-3400-2 (pbk.) — ISBN 978-1-4358-3401-9 (6-pack)
  1. San Antonio Spurs (Basketball team—History—Juvenile literature. I. Title.
  GV885.52.S26M33 2010
  796.323'6409764351—dc22
                                    2009009588

Manufactured in the United States of America

CONTENTS

THE LITTLE MARKET THAT COULD

San Antonio, Texas, is not one of the biggest cities in the United States. However, it has one of the most successful basketball teams. The San Antonio Spurs are one of the greatest basketball teams in the National Basketball Association, or NBA. Some sports fans believe that only **big-market teams** can have successful sports teams. The Spurs have proved them wrong.

Some of the best basketball players of all time have played for the San Antonio Spurs. Spurs players George Gervin, David Robinson, Tim Duncan, and Tony Parker are among the biggest stars the NBA has ever seen.

Tony Parker (center) joined the Spurs in 2001. He later became the team's starting point guard. Parker is known for being very fast.

COWBOY BOOTS

The Spurs got their name because their home is in Texas. Texas is known for its cowboys. Cowboys used to wear star-shaped metal objects called spurs on their boots. The cowboys poked the horses that they rode with spurs to make the animals run faster.

San Antonio is not a very big city, and the Spurs are the only major sports team in town. This makes for very **loyal** fans. Some people think San Antonio has the best fan base in America. The Spurs play their home games at San Antonio's AT&T Center. It is named after the telephone company AT&T. The team's colors are black and silver.

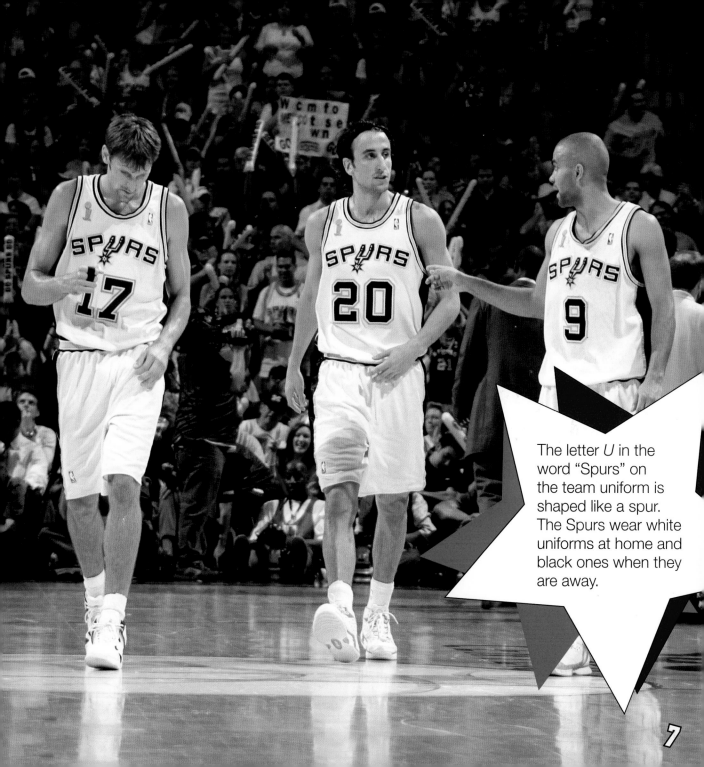

The letter *U* in the word "Spurs" on the team uniform is shaped like a spur. The Spurs wear white uniforms at home and black ones when they are away.

THE CHAPARRALS

The Spurs did not always play in San Antonio, and they were not always called the Spurs. The team began in 1967 as the Chaparrals. A chaparral is a group of thick bushes that grow in Texas. The Chaparrals were based in Dallas, Texas.

The Chaparrals were not very good. They were also not very **popular**. The team briefly changed its name from the Dallas Chaparrals to the Texas Chaparrals in the hopes of getting fans from all over the state. However, this did not help the team win more fans. Then, in 1973, a group of 36 San Antonio business leaders made a deal to bring the team to San Antonio.

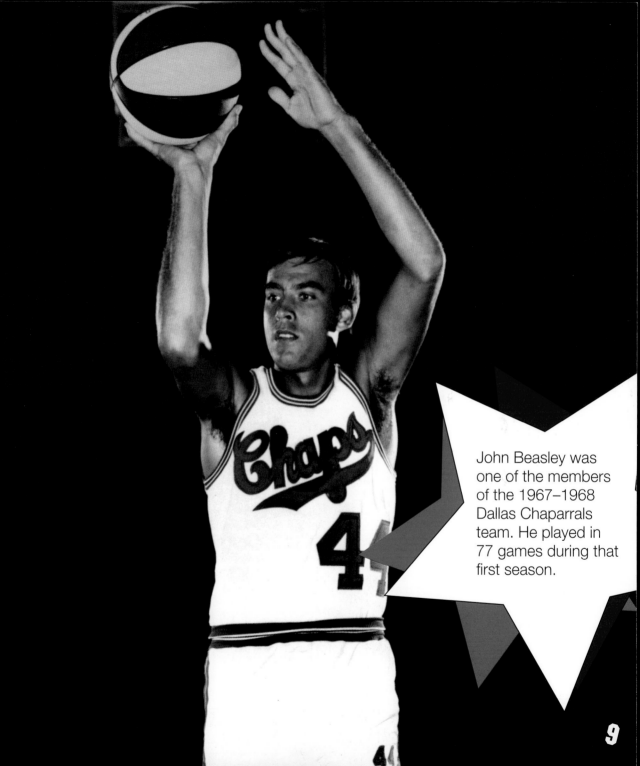

John Beasley was one of the members of the 1967–1968 Dallas Chaparrals team. He played in 77 games during that first season.

THE ICEMAN

The new owners decided that their team needed a better name. Who wanted to **root** for a team named after bushes? They almost named them the San Antonio Gunslingers, but then they decided on the Spurs. The move was just what the team needed. San Antonio basketball fans came out in big numbers to root for their new team.

One of basketball's biggest stars became a Spur in 1974. His name was George Gervin, and his nickname was the Iceman. He was called this because he was calm and cool on the court. Gervin led the Spurs to become one of the NBA's top teams in the 1977–1978 season. He scored more points than any other NBA player in that season.

George Gervin led the league in scoring for four seasons. That means he scored more points than any other player did during those seasons.

HELP FROM THE NAVY

The Spurs began to struggle after Gervin left the team in 1984. They needed a new superstar to bring the team together. The Spurs were so bad in the 1980s that it looked like they might have to move to another city.

Then, San Antonio found its new star in the 1987 NBA **Draft**. The Spurs picked a player from the United States **Naval Academy** named David Robinson. The Spurs would have to wait for their new player because Robinson had a two-year **commitment** to serve in the Navy. However, it was worth the wait. Robinson joined the team in 1989, and the Spurs went from last place to first place in the NBA.

Robinson became a huge star for the Spurs. In 1995, he was named the NBA's most valuable player, or MVP.

13

THE TWIN TOWERS

Robinson and the Spurs were good enough to make the **play-offs** in the 1990s. However, they kept losing before they could reach the NBA Finals. The Finals are the NBA's **championship**.

In 1997, Robinson was joined by another superstar, named Tim Duncan. Duncan had an excellent **rookie** season in 1997–1998. He was even voted Rookie of the Year. Robinson and Duncan were nicknamed the Twin Towers because they were both tall, skilled players. The Twin Towers led the Spurs to the Finals in 1999. The Spurs beat the New York Knicks and won San Antonio's long-awaited first championship.

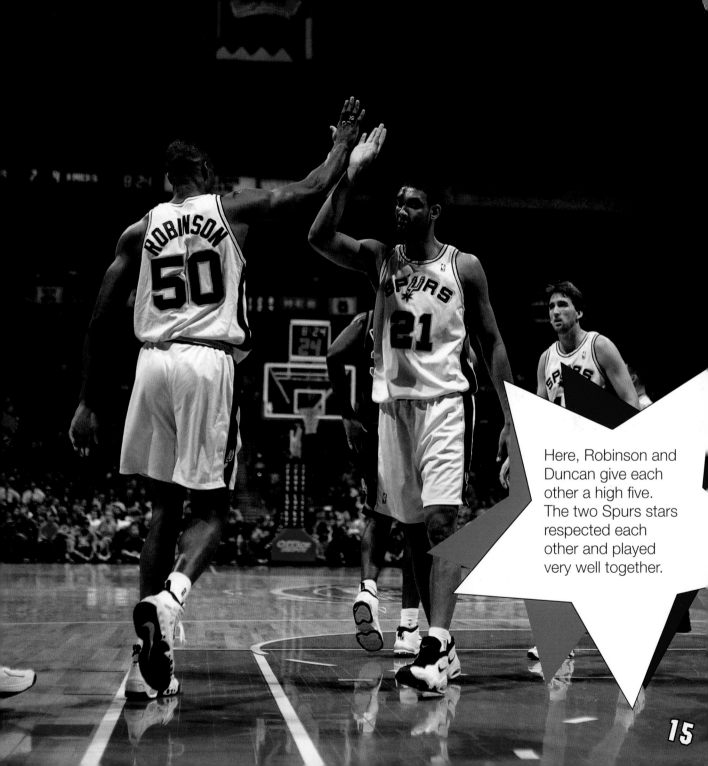

Here, Robinson and Duncan give each other a high five. The two Spurs stars respected each other and played very well together.

AN INTERNATIONAL TEAM

David Robinson decided that he would **retire** at the end of the 2002–2003 season. The Spurs **rallied** around their leader for his final chance to win another championship.

Even young Spurs players Tony Parker and Manu Ginóbili played well that season. Parker and Ginóbili are not from the United States. Parker is French, and Ginóbili is from Argentina. They prove that basketball is an **international** sport.

The Spurs won the 2003 Finals championship against the New Jersey Nets, and Robinson retired on top. Two years later, the Spurs returned to the Finals and beat the Detroit Pistons. It was San Antonio's third championship in just seven years!

Manu Ginóbili joined the Spurs during the 2002–2003 season. He is known for playing very well in the last few minutes of close games.

COMMUNITY TEAM

The people of San Antonio love their basketball team. The famous River Walk follows the San Antonio River as it flows through the city. The whole city throws a party on the River Walk when the Spurs win a championship. The Spurs players float down the river and wave to their fans. It is like a parade on boats.

Spurs fans also value the work that Spurs players have done in their community. David Robinson created a school in San Antonio called the Carver Academy. It is named after the American **scientist** George Washington Carver. The Iceman, George Gervin, formed the George Gervin Youth Center, which helps troubled children.

This boat is one of the many that floated down the San Antonio River to celebrate the Spurs' championship win in June 2005.

A BRIGHT FUTURE

The Spurs continue to play excellent basketball. They faced LeBron James and the Cleveland Cavaliers in the 2007 NBA Finals. James is one of the NBA's best players, but he and the Cavaliers never stood a chance against the Spurs. San Antonio **swept** Cleveland, 4–0.

The Spurs have some of the most famous players in basketball. San Antonio might be a small market, but it is world famous thanks to great players, such as Duncan, Parker, and Ginóbili. San Antonio fans know that their basketball team is here to stay. There are likely to be many more boat trips on the San Antonio River in the **future**.

The Spurs were full of joy and pride when they won their fourth NBA championship on June 14, 2007.

SAN ANTONIO SPURS TIMELINE

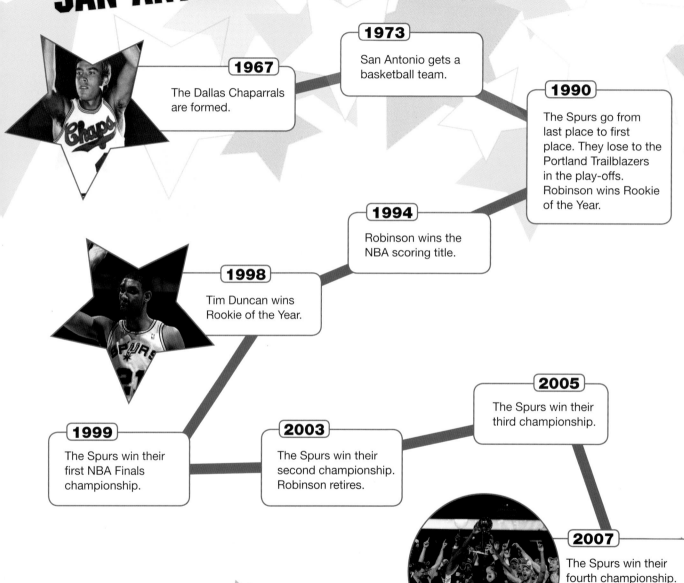

1967
The Dallas Chaparrals are formed.

1973
San Antonio gets a basketball team.

1990
The Spurs go from last place to first place. They lose to the Portland Trailblazers in the play-offs. Robinson wins Rookie of the Year.

1994
Robinson wins the NBA scoring title.

1998
Tim Duncan wins Rookie of the Year.

1999
The Spurs win their first NBA Finals championship.

2003
The Spurs win their second championship. Robinson retires.

2005
The Spurs win their third championship.

2007
The Spurs win their fourth championship.

GLOSSARY

BIG-MARKET TEAMS (big-MAR-ket TEEMZ) Teams based in large cities.

CHAMPIONSHIP (CHAM-pee-un-ship) Games held to decide the best, or the winner.

COMMITMENT (kuh-MIT-ment) A promise to do something.

DRAFT (DRAFT) The selection of people for a special purpose.

FUTURE (FYOO-chur) The time that is coming.

INTERNATIONAL (in-tur-NA-shuh-nul) Having to do with more than one country.

LOYAL (LOY-ul) True to a person or an idea.

NAVAL ACADEMY (NAY-vul uh-KA-deh-mee) A school for people who will be in the Navy. The Navy is made up of soldiers who fight at sea.

PLAY-OFFS (PLAY-ofs) Games played after the regular season ends to see who will play in the championship game.

POPULAR (PAH-pyuh-lur) Liked by lots of people.

RALLIED (RA-leed) Got back strength, power, or health.

RETIRE (rih-TY-ur) To give up an office or job.

ROOKIE (RU-kee) Having to do with a new major-league player.

ROOT (ROOT) To back a team or person.

SCIENTIST (SY-un-tist) A person who studies the world.

SWEPT (SWEPT) Won all stages of a game or series.

INDEX

WEB SITES

Due to the changing nature of Internet links, PowerKids Press has developed an online list of Web sites related to the subject of this book. This site is updated regularly. Please use this link to access the list:
www.powerkidslinks.com/teams/spur/